Instructor's Manual to Accompany

HOW ENGLISH WORKS

A Grammar Handbook with Readings

Ann Raimes

Hunter College, City University of New York

CAMBRIDGE
UNIVERSITY PRESS

# CAMBRIDGE
## UNIVERSITY PRESS

32 Avenue of the Americas, New York NY 10013-2473, USA

Published in the United States of America by Cambridge University Press, New York

Cambridge University Press is part of the University of Cambridge.

It furthers the University's mission by disseminating knowledge in the pursuit of education, learning and research at the highest international levels of excellence.

www.cambridge.org
Information on this title: www.cambridge.org/9780521657570

© Cambridge University Press 1998

First published by St. Martin's Press, Inc. 1990
18th printing 2012
Reprinted 2013

*A catalogue record for this publication is available from the British Library*

*Library of Congress Cataloguing in Publication data*

ISBN 978-0-521-65757-0 Paperback

# CONTENTS

TEACHING HOW ENGLISH WORKS

## The Approach of How English Works

How English Works approaches the study of the English language through what students see when they read. As students read in English—and most of them read a lot—they are faced by English in action, visible grammar. It is there on the page for them to notice, analyze, draw inferences from, and hypothesize about. The approach here is that students are encouraged to read, to use readings as a rich source of information about not only the style and rhetoric of English but its grammar and syntax as well. They begin with and use real texts: excerpts from nonfiction, newspapers, magazines, and textbooks; they are not limited to example sentences about "John and Mary." After using this book to dig deep into printed texts for information about the English language, students carry this technique with them as they read more. They develop habits of inquiry, of questioning, of associating what they see with what they know.

Many grammar books emphasize spoken English. However, when students speak English outside a classroom, they have very little opportunity to pause to analyze what they say, or to apply principles. They concentrate, quite rightly, on communicating their message to a listener. Writing gives students more chance to apply grammatical principles since a written text is instantly available for scrutiny, revision, and correction. They can monitor it at will until they feel they have got it right. So How English Works uses writing as well as reading, and written exercises as well as spoken exercises. It includes examples of authentic student writing to edit, and gives editing advice for the grammatical feature of each chapter.

## Using How English Works in the Classroom

The book has two parts, so it allows for different emphases. Instructors who teach a grammar course, prepare students for the TOEFL, or emphasize a comprehensive knowledge of English grammar as a basis for accurate writing can work their way systematically through the grammar chapters in Part I. Instructors who want to expose their students to as much reading and writing as possible, with grammar work included for the purposes of reading comprehension and editing writing can use the reading and writing tasks in Part II as the basic text, turning to the grammar chapters for explanation, reinforcement, and practice whenever necessary. These two options are outlined below.

## Beginning with Grammar

The chapters are organized so that students can build up a clear set of principles about the basic sentence, its parts (nouns, verbs, etc.), and then more complex variations of sentence coordination and subordination. If you use the chapters in order (obviously omitting any that are too easy or not necessary for your students' purposes), you have the choice of deciding whether to use only the reading excerpt that introduces the chapter, or to ask students to read the whole passage in Part II. If you decide on the latter (and students often find it helpful to have the excerpt put into its larger context), your students can read the whole passage as a homework assignment either before or after they read the grammar chapter excerpt. The passages are glossed, so reading one to three pages should not present a formidable obstacle, especially since the object of the reading is simply to understand the writer's point and to be exposed to the full context of the features of written English: grammar, syntax, vocabulary, idioms, spelling, punctuation, style, and rhetorical organization.

## Beginning with Reading and Writing

You might not have enough time or enough hours of instruction a week to be able to cover all the grammatical features in the twenty-nine chapters included here. In that case, you can begin by selecting a few reading passages in Part II, working through some or all of the additional material on each reading included in this manual (Preview Questions, Response Questions, and Analysis), and then assigning one writing task for each reading. From what the students write, you can select the areas of grammatical difficulty that they need to work on. You can determine priorities, and then you can turn to appropriate grammar chapters that address those difficulties. According to your teaching preference, you can work on a grammar chapter with the whole class; if you use group work successfully, you could have one group work on, say, subject-verb agreement while another works on pronoun reference.

With this approach, a student who has no difficulty at all with the use of articles will not be confused by explanations and exercises. Students who understand and use a grammatical feature accurately will then not have to spend classroom time on it. Once your students have read two or three of the passages in Part II, written about them, studied any appropriate grammar chapters, and worked on revisions, you (or the students) can then select the next few readings that the class will address. And once again, their needs, as demonstrated in their writing, will determine which grammar chapters will be useful.

If you adopt this second approach, you might find a checklist useful to indicate two or three error types according to the grammar chapter titles in this book. You can duplicate the Response Form and Checklist that appears on p. 5 to attach to your students' papers to show them in which paragraphs of their drafts the main problems occur and to direct them to specific pages and exercises in this book.

### Teaching the Grammar Chapters

Each grammar chapter has five sections: Read, Analyze, Study, Edit, and Write. Read the introductory reading passage with the class and ask students to do the Analyze tasks, either in groups, individually, or in whole-class discussion. You will see from the students' reactions which areas they have problems with, what they need to study and practice further. The Study section contains explanations, often with charts and diagrams, examples, and a lot of exercises. A class or an individual student might not need to study the whole section in detail or do every exercise. The instructor can select which points need to be studied, and which exercises will be of most help to the students. If students need some tasks to consolidate the work of the chapter, they can be asked to edit the piece of student writing in class, individually or in groups, or as a homework assignment. In addition, they can be asked to do the writing assignment, paying special attention to applying the editing guidelines. For this piece of writing, the students' attention should be directed first to generating ideas and content through writing, and then to accuracy through careful proofreading and application of the editing guidelines.

This manual contains an answer key to the exercises in the Study section. No answer key appears for the Analyze and Edit sections, since these answers are often more open-ended, with a variety of alternatives.

Note that throughout this section, a five-pointed star indicates a linguistically challenging exercise. A sentence with an asterisk is a sentence that is NOT grammatically acceptable. It is essential that students be made aware of this; otherwise, they might regard a sentence in print as a sentence to be copied!

## Teaching the Readings

Each reading passage is glossed to make it easy for students to read quickly with good comprehension. Instructors who want to spend class time on using the readings to stimulate class discussion and to examine the writer's rhetorical choices will find additional sections in this manual: Preview Questions, Response Questions, and Analysis. Those who want to concentrate on grammar in class time can ask students to read the passage and then do the writing assignment at home; class time can then be devoted to studying the grammar chapters that the instructor finds appropriate after reading and analyzing the students' writing. Students can be asked to revise the written assignment and to pay special attention to the grammar area in question. Or, if the content and organization of the first draft is acceptable, students can be asked simply to rewrite the draft with corrections of errors and/or rewriting of problem sentences.

Each reading is accompanied by a list of the grammar chapters in which excerpts are used to form examples and exercises. An instructor can thus see at a glance which grammatical points the reading connects with in the book.

## Dealing with Errors

It is always hard to know exactly what to do with errors in our students' writing. We are trained to recognize errors, and we seem to feel that to show we know our job, we have to find and correct every error on every paper. Yet research into second language acquisition and pedagogy shows us that such approaches are not always productive: we need to determine the purpose of our marking, what the students are to do next, and how they understand and react to our feedback. If we are looking at a first draft of a piece of writing that will be revised for ideas and organization, we might decide to concentrate far less on grammatical correction than we would if we were looking either at a third draft in which the student was specifically working on producing accurate forms for an academic audience, or at a final exam intended to judge a student's mastery of grammatical principles.

This is advice I would give on how to handle the marking of writing that students do as they use this book:

1.  For writing tasks that follow the readings in Part II, begin by making comments on ideas and organization. Look for and comment on strengths, in terms of both ideas and language use. On the first or second draft, draw students' attention to the main one, two, or three grammatical problems that show up in specific paragraphs in their writing and refer them to grammar chapters or exercises as necessary. You can use the <u>Response Form and Checklist</u> on p. 5 for this purpose. After students have studied a chapter or done a few exercises, indicate in the margin of their revision and of any further assignments whenever they make an error of that type and ask them to correct the error. Gradually, the students build up a repertory of grammatical areas that they have studied and are expected to edit for before they present a piece of writing to a reader.

2.  For writing done in response to open-ended (no one "right answer") tasks that occur in the grammar chapters in Part I, such as the tasks in the <u>Write</u> section of each chapter, check every correct response and circle every error that is covered in the chapter. If a student has used one correct form and one incorrect form within one or two sentences, let the correct form serve as a model:

I <u>could have</u> changed my job and I <u>could have</u> make a lot more money.

Ask the student to correct it. Either ignore or correct any other errors that occur, depending upon your aims and your students' needs, level, and ability, but make sure that your students know which policy you have decided on, and why.

3. For single-sentence "right-answer" grammar exercises, ask students to form pairs or small groups to compare their versions and make sure that they are the same. If they are not, then the students have to try to justify to each other why they chose one particular response. Or ask students to correct each other's papers as you lead the class through giving the correct responses.

RESPONSE FORM AND CHECKLIST, USING HOW ENGLISH WORKS

Student's name _____

Comments on ideas and organization:




Your main problem areas in grammar in this draft:

| Problem Area and Chapter | Paragraph # | Study Page(s) | Do Exercise(s) # |
|---|---|---|---|
| 1. Subject and predicate _____ | | | |
| 2. Phrases and clauses _____ | | | |
| 3. Questions and negatives _____ | | | |
| 4. Proper nouns _____ | | | |
| 5. Countable and uncountable nouns | | | |
| 6. Articles _____ | | | |
| 7. Verb phrases _____ | | | |
| 8. Verb tenses _____ | | | |
| 9. Past _____ | | | |
| 10. Present and future _____ | | | |
| 11. Modal auxiliaries _____ | | | |
| 12. Active and passive _____ | | | |
| 13. Verb forms (+ Appendix A) _____ | | | |
| 14. Adjectives _____ | | | |
| 15. Adverbs _____ | | | |
| 16. Comparisons _____ | | | |
| 17. Subject—verb agreement _____ | | | |
| 18. Pronouns and pronoun reference _____ | | | |
| 19. Infinitives _____ | | | |
| 20. -ing forms _____ | | | |
| 21. Participle forms _____ | | | |
| 22. Coordinating conjunctions _____ | | | |
| 23. Transitions _____ | | | |
| 24. Adjectival clauses _____ | | | |
| 25. Noun clauses and reported speech | | | |
| 26. Adverbial clauses _____ | | | |
| 27. Adverbial clauses: conditions _____ | | | |
| 28. Style _____ | | | |
| 29. Punctuation _____ | | | |
| Spelling (Appendix B) _____ | | | |

# Sources of Students' Errors

One very interesting way to approach errors, especially after the
students have studied a chapter, is to discuss with them why language
students make errors, and what the various sources of those errors are.  In
my classes, I circulate the following description and examples.  This
description of sources of errors was originally based on H. Douglas Brown's
categories in Principles of Language Learning and Teaching 2nd edition
(Englewood Cliffs, NJ: Prentice-Hall, 1987), but was then changed and added
to as my students contributed examples of their own.


## 1. Transfer from the native language

Transfer from a first language occurs mostly at the early stages of
learning a second language.  Researchers have found, though, that less th
25% of grammatical errors in adults' speech is due to transfer from L1.

Francoise wrote: six advices
Her explanation: "Advice is a countable noun in French and it's for this
reason I made this error."


## 2. Application of interlanguage rules

A major factor in second language learning is that learners make
generalizations of rules within the target language—and those
generalizations are often incorrect.  Learners form hypotheses about how
English works and build upon them. So they might say things like: "Does h
can sing?" or "They goed." A learner of French might say, "Il a tombé."

Martine wrote: How can this creates a problem?
Her explanation: "I used the wrong form after the modal auxiliary can. I
was using an −s on a verb in the third person (English rule!)"

Annick wrote: In contrast with United States, most European families stil
have the concept of those traditional meals around a table.
Her explanation: "The error is the lack of article in front of the countr
I made the error because a lot of countries in English language don't nee
an article."

Hui-Min wrote: Chinese New Year always gives us fun and exciting.
Her explanation: "I used wrong forms. After gives us have to follow nouns
fun and excitement. I thought exciting was a noun form because some verbs
add −ing form to become nouns. For example: He is getting used to living
New York. Living is a noun."

It is important to note that sometimes the way something is taught or is
presented in a textbook can lead students to make faulty generalizations
about the new language ("teacher-induced errors"!).

## 3. Use of communication strategies

Learners use different strategies to get a message across. When learners do not have the precise way of conveying an idea at their disposal in the target language, they will often use one of the following strategies:

### a. Avoidance

A Japanese student who did not know how to spell liar tried it a few times, and then crossed out the whole sentence: "He is a liar" and wrote instead: "He doesn't tell the true."

### b. Prefabricated patterns

Sometimes learners memorize phrases or sentences and then misuse them in context. One student knew the expression "on the contrary" but misused it in this sentence:

> My brother's room is messy. On the contrary, my sister's room is tidy.

### c. Reliance on previously used (and uncorrected) forms

Students who have heard and used certain expressions without ever having an error pointed out will develop an intuitive feeling that what they have so often heard and used is correct.

Sepehr wrote: Have you ever think about the causes of change in the family?
His explanation: "I made the mistake because when I talked in daily language I always said 'Have you ever think.' So it was something that I got used to it. By getting used to, I mean even when I saw it on the paper and I was correcting my mistakes I thought that the sentence should be wrong but when I repeat both of the sentences the first one seemed familiar and more correct. And with my background in my first language (in my language we have few words that people use them wrong, but because they are common mistakes, they use them even in the book) so I thought it might be one of those 'common mistakes'."

### d. Appeal to authority

A learner asks a native speaker or looks something up in a dictionary. One student tried to find an alternative for the word might and, after consulting a dictionary, wrote this sentence: "She power go back to her country next year."

### e. Cognitive and personality styles

Because of the way they think or the way their personalities operate, students might make mistakes in producing inappropriately formal or informal language. They might be very cautious, using only what they know in short simple sentences, or they might take risks and try to express complicated ideas in complex sentences.

## 4. Mistakes

Some errors are errors of performance only, since they do not reflect the student's underlying competence in the language. The student who writes ' been living here all my life" but reads out loud "I've been living here ε my life" has made a mistake of performance rather than an error arising from lack of competence.

———————

We discuss the handout at length, with students contributing their own examples that I include in handouts in later semesters. Then, as soon as the students have studied a grammar chapter, whenever an error of that type appears in their writing, I indicate by underlining that an error has occurred. Their task is to write what the error was and how they would correct it, and to speculate about what the source of that error was. In other words, they write answers to these questions:

What is the error?
How would you correct it?
Why do you think you made the error?

By doing this, students begin to see error as something interesting and intellectually engaging, not just a stigma. They see it as an essential and telling part of language learning.

## Preparing Students for Essay Examinations

Since grammatical accuracy in writing is frequently one of the demands of essay examinations for college applications, for the TOEFL Test of Written English, and for college courses, teaching students how to edit for grammatical accuracy becomes a part of instruction in writing. Many instructors will teach their students a variety of methods of generating ideas, organizing them, and revising. In addition to that, they have to teach them how to respond to an essay examination when there is no time allowed for prewriting or for revision. In such examinations, quick, efficient planning and organizing are essential, as are efficient proofreading techniques based on a sound and thorough knowledge of grammatical principles.

How English Works can be used to help students with essay examinations in the following way:

1. Make the writing tasks attached to the readings timed tasks. If necessary, adapt and modify the wording of the task so that it approximates the type of task the students will have to face.

2. Show students on the board how you would go about analyzing the wording of the question: pick out the key words, underline them, and write one sentence that begins "In this essay my reader expects me to . . ."

3. Show students how you would generate ideas quickly for an essay on an assigned topic. Show how you would jot down notes for each point of support, and how you would write down what examples and illustrations you would include to develop a paragraph.

4. Discuss with the students what would be effective ways to begin and end an essay.

5. Hand out samples of student essays: analyze them for content and organization. Ask students to make a paragraph by paragraph summary, one sentence for each paragraph. Ask students what the writer is saying in each paragraph and what details the writer offers as evidence for what he or she says.

6. Hand out samples of student essays or project them with an overhead projector. Show the students what careful proofreading entails: read one line at a time with a sheet of paper blocking out the rest of the page; read the last sentence first and work backwards through the essay; examine every verb and check it for tense, form, and agreement with its subject; examine every problem area (e.g. articles, spelling).

7. Emphasize how necessary it is for students to become familiar with the principles of English grammar in order to edit effectively. How English Works will help.

PART I: ANSWER KEY TO EXERCISES

There is often more than one correct answer to an item in an exercise. One answer is given here. Make sure that students consult with you if they have another answer that they think is correct.

## CHAPTER 1: Subject and Predicate

### Exercise 1

1. X—Everything was nice and clean.
2. OK
3. X—No verb in second sentence
4. X—No independent clause in second sentence
5. OK
6. X—Second sentence has no verb.
7. X—Second sentence has no verb.
8. X—Second sentence has no subject and no verb; it should be connected to the first sentence.

### Exercise 3

Omitted verb phrases:

the sheets and pillows [are] very light greenish lemon
The coverlet [is] scarlet.
The window [is] green.
The toilet-table [is] orange.
The basin [is] blue.
The doors [are] lilac.

### Exercise 5

1. Last year,
2. Also,
3. Years ago, when I lived in a two-room apartment,
4. Sometimes
5. Every time I walk from the bedroom or the study to the kitchen
6. When I was growing up,

### Exercise 6

1. The big chair is very comfortable.
2. . . . ; it has a lot of antique furniture.
3. The pictures that are on the walls around the room are mostly landscapes.
4. Buying expensive furniture has made . . . or Expensive furniture has made . . .
5. Then she wanted a new table, too.
6. The lamp on the table next to the window belonged to my grandmother.

Exercise 10

1. b. Omit they; the subject is big rooms.
2. b. Omit he; the subject is Mr. Johnson.
3. a. study
4. a. Omit by.
5. a. Omit they; the subject is The pictures.


## CHAPTER 2: Phrases and Clauses

### Exercise 5

1. The woman gave the man a smile.
   The woman gave a smile to the man.
2. Her sister lent her a sweater.
3. Pierre bought his girlfriend a ring.
   Pierre bought a ring for his girlfriend.
4. Marie told her boyfriend a lie.
   Marie told a lie to her boyfriend.
5. He taught his students everything he knew.
   He taught everything he knew to his students.
6. She made her sister a cake.
   She made a cake for her sister.


### Exercise 8

1. b
2. c
3. a
4. a
5. d


## CHAPTER 3: Questions and Negatives

### Exercise 1

1. Does he tell lies?
   How often does he tell lies?
2. Is she telling the truth?
   Why is she telling the truth?
3. Should doctors follow a code of ethics?
   Which code of ethics should doctors follow?
4. Has Dr. Jones concealed the truth?
   Who has concealed the truth?

5.  Has Dr. Smith concealed the truth, too?
    Why has Dr. Smith concealed the truth, too?
6.  Did the doctors try to be honest?
    What did the doctors try to do?


## Exercise 3

1.  Who(m) did she go to see?
2.  Why did she go to the doctor?
3.  When did she make the appointment?
4.  What did he tell her?
5.  How did she react?
6.  What did she tell the doctor about?
7.  Whose plan was it to increase productivity 50 percent?
8.  How many hours a day was she working?


## Exercise 5

1.  Why did the doctor tell his patient a lie?
    What did the doctor tell his patient a lie for?
2.  Why did the doctor order a set of X-rays?
    What did the doctor order a set of X-rays for?
3.  Why did the doctor test his reflexes?
    What did the doctor test his reflexes for?
4.  Why are the hospital employees on strike?
    What are the hospital employees on strike for?
5.  Why did he refuse to have an operation?
    What did he refuse to have an operation for?
6.  Why are the patients being sent home?
    What are the patients being sent home for?


## Exercise 6

1.  I didn't ever use the living room.
2.  . . . who didn't have any living-room furniture.
3.  I clearly have no clue . . .
4.  My living room doesn't have a clear function.
5.  There is no one in the room.
6.  There isn't ever any activity in the room.
7.  None of the explanations help.
8.  The room doesn't offer the family anything.


## Exercise 7

1.  They have never entertained in the living room.
2.  She seldom uses the living room.
3.  They rarely sit and talk in that room.
4.  I would never have expected such a disaster.
5.  They could never have predicted that crisis.
6.  He would not eat a mouthful for days on end.

Exercise 8
In the first sentence, has is used as a main verb, so we need to use the does auxiliary in the tag. In the second sentence, has is used as an auxiliary (with had the main verb—participle form), so the auxiliary is repeated in the tag.


Exercise 9

1. Yes, he will.
2. Yes, she is.
3. No, she isn't.
4. Yes, there are.
5. Yes, they do.
6. Yes, he did.
7. No, he doesn't.
8. Yes, they are.


Exercise 10

1. I have a nice living room, don't I?
2. People never sit in the living room, do they?
3. The room always looks neat and tidy, doesn't it?
4. It would not solve the problem, would it?
5. This would not solve the problem, would it?
6. Lillian had no living room furniture, did she?
7. I am too old to have a bed in the living room, aren't I?
8. Her mother had chosen the pool, hadn't she?
9. Lies do harm to those who tell them, don't they?
10. Doctors confront such choices often and urgently, don't they?
11. There is a need to debate this issue, isn't there?
12. The seriously ill do not want to know the truth, do they?


CHAPTER 4: Proper Nouns


Exercise 3

1. China, Japan, and the United States of America
2. the Chinese
3. Buddhism;   Japan
4. cotton
5. Coca-Cola;   Hong Kong
6. American;   soy oil
7. Mississippi
8. South America;   Brazil;   coffee


Exercise 4

West: singular, part of the globe

Carolus Linnaeus: singular, name of person
Holland: singular, country
New World: singular, part of globe
Samuel Bowen: singular, name of person
China: singular, country
Lauderdale County: singular, region
Tennessee: singular, state
Second World War: singular, historical event
China: singular, country
Chinese: plural, nationality
West: singular, part of the globe
U.S: plural, country
Europe: singular, continent
Japan: singular, country
United States: plural, name of country
Cinderella: singular, name of person

## CHAPTER 5: Countable and Uncountable Nouns

### Exercise 1

| Countable Singular | Countable Plural |
|---|---|
| approach | doctors |
| need | patients |
| promise | lines |
| interest | requirements |
| man | needs |
| checkup | doctors |
| family | months |
| form | doctors |
| prognosis | doctors |
| vacation | choices |
| patient | times |
| | reasons |
| | eyes |
| | lies |

### Exercise 2

| Noun | Common/ Proper | Countable/ Uncountable | Singular/ Plural |
|---|---|---|---|
| Lillian | P | | |
| house | C | C | S |
| Beverly Hills | P | | |
| living room | C | C | S |
| mother | C | C | S |
| trouble | C | U | |
| schemes | C | C | P |

| days | C | C | P |
|------|---|---|---|
| Arlene | P | | |
| choice | C | C | S |
| furniture | C | U | |
| pool | C | C | S |

## Exercise 3

Dictionary plural: tomatoes, radios, pianos, potatoes, heroes, spies, feet, geese, oxen, analyses, crises, formulae/formulas, alumni, sheep, shelves

## Exercise 5

1. [My mother] was a magician at stretching a dollar.
         C              C           C

2. Doris was in the kitchen when I barged into her bedroom
                    C                         C
   one afternoon in search of a safety pin.
        C         U            C

3. Since her bedroom opened onto a community hallway, she
            C                     C
   kept the door locked, but needing the pin, I took the
         C                    C
   key from its hiding place, unlocked the door, and
   C               C              C
   stepped in.

4. I was overwhelmed by the discovery that she had
                             C
   squandered such money on me and sickened by the
                U
   knowledge that, bursting into her room like this, I had
     U                       C
   robbed her of the pleasure of seeing me astonished and
                           C
   delighted.

5. [It] made me feel as though I'd struck a blow against
                                    C
   her happiness.
       U

## Exercise 6

1. b or c
2. c
3. a or d
4. a or b or c
5. b or c or d

## Exercise 7

1. The world surrounding us affects us in a more or less direct way <u>or</u> in more or less direct ways.
2. We are affected by our surroundings, like furniture and colors.
3. Dark and crowded rooms make me upset.
4. She bought a lot of new furniture for her room.
5. Every student likes to have a quiet place to study.
6. My brother has a large number of friends.
7. Rice is an important crop in my country.
8. He bought some new pants last week.
9. That pair of gloves belongs to my mother.
10. The homework we had last week took a very long time.
11. I have fewer opportunities for practice than other students in my class.
12. They don't have many possibilities for promotion.


## CHAPTER 6: Articles

### Exercise 1

the knowledge—within text: refers to "that I had robbed her," etc.
the pleasure—within text: refers to "of seeing me astonished and delighted"
the key—familiar: the key to the bedroom door
the slightest hint—with superlative
the least word—with superlative
the faintest intonation—with superlative
the weakest gesture—with superlative
the happiness—within text: refers to "of seeing me stunned with amazement"


### Exercise 2

*Bicycle is useful.
A singular countable noun must have a determiner preceding it.


### Exercise 3

Countable plural: <u>conflicts, Patients, answers, alternatives, hospitals, believers</u>
Uncountable: <u>treatment, information, deception</u>


### Exercise 5

| Noun Phrase | Count. | Uncount. | Sing. | Pl. | Specific | Nonspecific |
|---|---|---|---|---|---|---|
| work | | ✓ | | | | |
| the kitchen | ✓ | | ✓ | | ✓ | |
| a safety pin | ✓ | | ✓ | | | ✓ |

| | Count. | Uncount. | Sing. | Pl. | Specific | Nonspecific |
|---|---|---|---|---|---|---|
| a community hallway | ✓ | | ✓ | | | ✓ |
| the door | ✓ | | ✓ | | ✓ | |
| the pin | ✓ | | ✓ | | ✓ | |
| the key | ✓ | | ✓ | | ✓ | |
| a big, black bicycle | ✓ | | ✓ | | | ✓ |
| a Baltimore shop window | ✓ | | ✓ | | | ✓ |
| the price | ✓ | | ✓ | | ✓ | |
| a down payment | ✓ | | ✓ | | | ✓ |
| the bicycle | ✓ | | ✓ | | ✓ | |

## Exercise 6

a.  the  
b.  the  
c.  the  
d.  the  
e.  the  
f.  the  
g.  a  
h.  the  
i.  a  
j.  a (the also acceptable)  

k.  the  
l.  a (the also acceptable)  
m.  the  
n.  the  
o.  the  
p.  the  
q.  the  
r.  the  
s.  the  

## Exercise 7

1. d.  the prettiest room.
2. b.  furniture or any furniture
3. b.  the only thing
4. d.  a pool
5. b.  the end
6. d.  any of the hopes

## Exercise 8

1. a.  The
   b.  Zero article
2. a.  The
   b.  Zero article
3. a.  Zero article
   b.  The
4. a.  Zero article
   b.  The
5. a.  The
   b.  Zero article

6.  a.  Zero article
    b.  The
7.  a.  a
    b.  the
8.  a.  The
    b.  Zero article


## CHAPTER 7: Verb Phrases

### Exercises 1 and 2

1. (The couches) were recently cleaned by men with small machines.

2. (Many reasons) have been put forward for why (we) never use the living room.

3. (Sharp conflicts) are now arising.

4. What should (doctors) say to a 46-year-old man?

5. (Bean curd) has been made in China for 2,000 years.

6. As we talked, walking through the corridors of plane trees (that) line the streets of Shanghai, (we) would pass through the outdoor markets.

### Exercise 3

|     | Active | Passive |
| --- | --- | --- |
| 1. | exists | must be made |
| 2. | reflects | |
| 3. | | are engaged |
| 4. | | can be divided |
| 5. | does serve | |
| 6. | | is recognized |
| 7. | | are sold |
| 8. | has run out | |

### Exercise 4

Present-future verbs:
which read like a continuous diary (Although read has the same form for
    past, the present meaning is more likely here.)
are among the most moving
can feel the artist's sense of mission
become aware of the immense strain

The author uses the present cluster in these cases because he is describing
our perceptions of the artist from his letters when we read them now.

## Exercise 5

were made: past (early 1960's)
were: past
was: past
was invented: past
is: present (it still is now)
is: present
serves: present
contains: present
have helped: present
continues: present
is: present


## Exercise 6

1. b
2. d
3. c
4. d
5. a


## Exercise 7

| Subject | Verb Phrase | Active/Passive | Time Cluster |
|---|---|---|---|
| that vegetable | is | A | present |
| the Western diet | is built | P | present |
| I | had traveled | A | past |
| the whole story | began | A | past |
| farmers | started | A | past |
| they | did | A | past |
| why [they did this] | is | A | present |
| that | lie | A | present |
| plants | are | A | present |
| the seeds | are | A | present |
| the farmers | persevered | A | past |
| evidence | suggests | A | present |
| the soybean | had been taught | P | past |
| These changes | were | A | past |
| The new crop | arrived | A | past |
| The bean | is | A | present |
| The bean | grows | A | present |
| The soybean plant | supports | A | present |
| that | return | A | present |
| this | was | A | past |
| that | had been farming | A | past |
| farmers | had | A | past |
| The enthusiasm | is suggested | P | present |

# CHAPTER 8: Verb Tenses: Overview

## Exercise 2

1. d
2. a
3. c
4. b
5. a
6. c

## Exercise 3

1. has been (he is still alive)
   was (he is no longer alive)
2. cooked
3. bought
4. has owned (she still owns it)
   owned (she no longer owns it)
5. has not found
6. has made
7. had
8. have not had, walked

## Exercise 4

1. They were in the middle of leaving. They were putting on their coats and saying goodbye. They began leaving at 9:55.
2. The room was empty. Nobody was there. They had left at 9:30.
3. People saw me and decided to leave! They began leaving at 10:02. I worried that I caused them to leave.

## Exercise 6

1. seem
2. contained
3. is wearing
4. needs
5. belongs
6. are trying
7. own, looks
8. prefers

## Exercise 7

1. was hitting
2. had been fighting
3. are probably sleeping
4. has been trying
5. will have been playing
6. had been fighting

## Exercise 8

a.  met
b.  was <u>or</u> is
c.  met
d.  danced
e.  started
f.  lived
g.  worked
h.  used to
i.  saw
j.  lives
k.  has
l.  pays
m.  has
n.  is
o.  is

## CHAPTER 9: Verb Tenses: Past

### Exercise 1

| | |
|---|---|
| had walked | past perfect |
| did not see | basic past |
| was | basic past |
| had bicycled | past perfect |
| had met | past perfect |
| found | basic past |
| started | basic past |
| passed | basic past |
| finished | basic past |
| heard | basic past |
| looked | basic past |
| noticed | basic past |
| limped | basic past |
| got | basic past |
| could see | modal |
| was | basic past |
| was set | past (passive) |
| was | basic past |
| saw | basic past |
| came | basic past |
| squatted | basic past |
| explained | basic past |
| had returned | past perfect |
| said | basic past |
| asked | basic past |
| was doing | past progressive |
| showed | basic past |
| lit up | basic past |
| cupped | basic past |

| | |
|---|---|
| yelled | basic past |
| appeared | basic past |
| let | basic present |
| said | basic past |
| dragged | basic past |

## Exercise 2

a. have often exchanged
b. remember
c. was
d. went
e. didn't know or did not know
f. got
g. seemed
h. seemed
i. danced
j. cried
k. saw
l. finished
m. clapped
n. gave
o. made
p. was

## Exercise 4

1. There was once a frontier mining town where 100 miners were employed in the town's only basic industry—gold mining. Each of the miners was married and had two children. The basic industry thus supported 400 people.

2. But the 400 people demanded services: schools and churches had to be built, grocery and clothing stores and livery stables were operated, newspapers were published, professional personnel were needed, and saloons had to cater to visiting cowboys.

3. With 100 miners, this community supported 300 people in the various nonbasic service industries.

4. The basic mining industry not only supported its own 300 dependents but also economically supported the 300 nonbasic personnel and their 900 dependents, for a grand total of 1,600 people.

## Exercise 7

1. had eaten
2. enjoyed
3. gave
4. had hurt
5. got
6. had given

**CHAPTER 10: Verb Tenses: Present and Future**

## Exercise 2

| Subject | Singular/Plural | Verb |
|---|---|---|
| Many business people | P | show |
| he | S | points out |
| dim lighting, subdued noise levels, and comfortable seats | P | encourage |
| (business) that | S | tries |
| Sommer | S | describes |
| the uncomfortable chairs | P | make |
| (students) who | P | sit |
| those next to the teacher | P | avoid |
| the middle of the first row | S | contains |
| (students) who | P | interact |
| we | P | move |
| interaction | S | decreases |

## Exercise 4

1. left
2. have wanted
3. decided
4. have written
5. bought
6. have completed

## Exercise 5

1. c
2. a
3. c
4. b
5. c

## Exercise 7

1. b.  feels
2. a.  will have been married
3. a.  are trying
4. a.  have been studying

# CHAPTER 11: Modal Auxiliaries

## Exercise 2

Possible answers:
1. Would you please put out your cigarette?
2. Do you think you could stop talking, please?
3. Could I please borrow your book? or Would you please lend me your book?
4. Would you mind lending me $20?
5. Would you mind playing that record again?
6. May I please squeeze in?

## Exercise 5

1. He should have sent a message.
2. She should have taken her medicine.
3. They should have written their letters.
4. He should have driven carefully.
5. She should have paid her credit card bills.

## Exercise 10

Possible answers:
1. a. It is prohibited. The machine will give you an electric shock.
   b. You are allowed to, but it's not necessary. (You have only one item to wash.)
2. a. That's my advice. You're not doing well, and I never see you in the library.
   b. It is essential—otherwise, we won't pay your tuition any more.
3. a. It's possible that it is. There's a chance that it is.
   b. I have evidence to show that it is. Everyone else agrees with him.
4. a. But she didn't—so now she can't go on vacation with us.
   b. I don't know if she has enough. It's possible.
   c. She never seems to spend anything, so I assume she has saved her money.
   d. She has very rich parents who pay for her. She spends everything she earns.
   e. She had a lot of medical bills and was in debt. The only way she could pay was to save most of her salary.
5. a. I am sure that that is what will happen: he is usually punctual.
   b. The traffic isn't bad today, and he left early enough. So I expect he will be on time.
   c. I don't know if the traffic is bad or not. And I don't know when he left. It's possible that he will be on time, but I can't be sure.
6. a. She was sick. She left work early for a reason.
   b. She looks very sick. She hasn't seen a doctor yet. I think it would help her.

**CHAPTER 12: Active and Passive**

Exercise 1

1. are. defined
2. were asked
3. prevents
4. have been delayed
5. lie
6. be studying or study

Exercise 2

1. Supplies were delivered to the North Pole last week.
2. New tax laws were passed . . .
3. The defense budget will be revised . . .
4. Rice is grown . . .
5. The soybean is cultivated . . .
6. My sweater was made . . .
7. The game should be cancelled . . .
8. That course might have been offered . . .

Exercise 3

The author chose the following clause or sentence:

1. a
2. a
3. a
4. a
5. b
6. a
7. b

Exercise 5

1. The stockholders were sent copies of the takeover bid.
   Copies of the takeover bid were sent to the stockholders.
2. She was handed a set of instructions.
   A set of instructions was handed to her.
3. The boss was told the whole story of the takeover attempt.
   The whole story of the takeover attempt was told to the boss.
4. The reporters were given the information.
   The information was given to the reporters.
5. The chief executive was paid a huge amount of money.
   A huge amount of money was paid to the chief executive.

| Exercise 6 | Exercise 7 |
|---|---|
| 1. being | 1. c |
| 2. been | 2. a |
| 3. being | 3. c |
| 4. been | 4. d |
| 5. being | 5. b |
| 6. been | 6. d |
| | 7. c |

## CHAPTER 13: Verb Forms: Summary

### Exercise 1

| Main verb | Auxiliary |
|---|---|
| were | are shaped (participle) |
| were | was furnished (participle) |
| are | were asked (participle) |
| is | were judging (-ing) |
| 's (is) | |
| was | |
| were | |
| isn't | |
| 're (are) | |

### Exercises 2 and 3

| Verb Phrase | Past | Present-Future | Active | Passive |
|---|---|---|---|---|
| 1. had walked | ✓ | | ✓ | |
| did see | ✓ | | ✓ | |
| was | ✓ | | ✓ | |
| had bicycled | ✓ | | ✓ | |
| had met | ✓ | | ✓ | |
| found | ✓ | | ✓ | |
| started | ✓ | | ✓ | |
| 2. was attracting | ✓ | | ✓ | |
| was working | ✓ | | ✓ | |
| left | ✓ | | ✓ | |

| Verb Phrase | Past | Present-Future | Active | Passive |
|---|---|---|---|---|
| 3. was told | ✓ | | | ✓ |
| was | ✓ | | ✓ | |
| were grown | ✓ | | | ✓ |
| was raised | ✓ | | | ✓ |
| was | ✓ | | ✓ | |
| were attended to | ✓ | | | ✓ |
| had been taken care of | ✓ | | | ✓ |
| 4. have been put forward | | ✓ | | ✓ |
| use | | ✓ | ✓ | |
| came to believe | ✓ | | ✓ | |
| was | ✓ | | ✓ | |
| got | ✓ | | ✓ | |
| are | | ✓ | ✓ | |
| make | | ✓ | ✓ | |
| is | | ✓ | ✓ | |
| don't use | | ✓ | ✓ | |
| are feeling | | ✓ | ✓ | |
| wander | | ✓ | ✓ | |
| admire | | ✓ | ✓ | |

## Exercise 4

a. dedicated
b. been
c. said
d. do
e. tested
f. devoted

## Exercise 5

1. c. were judging
2. c. was given
3. d. had signed
4. d. didn't remember
5. a. is occupied
6. c. might have moved

## CHAPTER 14: Adjectives and Noun Modifiers

### Exercise 1

Most occurred before a noun. Those occurring after a linking verb were <u>was</u> <u>late</u>, <u>were</u> <u>visible</u>, <u>looked</u> <u>dusty</u> <u>and</u> <u>dry</u>, and <u>is</u> <u>average</u>.

### Exercise 5

1. the table top
2. the windshield wipers
3. the door locks
4. a shopping cart
5. a jewelry box
6. a cookie jar
7. a pencil case
8. a change purse
9. a flower bed
10. an economics book
11. orange peel
12. a dessert tray

### Exercise 6

1. He made a last-minute request.
2. She has a blue-eyed, fair-haired daughter.
3. There will be a twenty-minute delay.
4. She wrote a ten-page report.
5. They want to hire a hard-working secretary.
6. They bought a sixty-year-old house.
7. She has a three-legged cat.
8. He provided a well-cooked meal.
9. They bought a high-priced car.
10. We needed a ten-foot-long rope to get the cat out of the tree.

### Exercise 7

1. puzzling
2. puzzled
3. excited
4. frightening
5. annoying
6. exciting

### Exercise 8

minute: size
electronic: material

plastic: material
lamp: qualifier

subdued: observation
noise: qualifier

absorbent: observation
building: qualifier

empty: observation
rectangular: shape

bare: observation
cement: material

big: size
black: color


## Exercise 11

1. The data stolen from the computer lab were being used in a medical experiment.
2. The footprints found in the dust gave the police a clue.
3. They collected new data suitable for use in the experiment.
4. The only door open was the metal security door.
5. The only person agile enough to climb over the fence was the chief engineer.
6. The young police detective, eager for promotion, asked to take over the case.
7. Dissatisfied with the evidence, the detective recalled the two key witnesses.
8. Called to the witness stand, the witnesses had to testify.


## CHAPTER 15: Adverbs and Frequency Adverbs


## Exercise 1

1. Just add -ly: usual + -ly = usually
2. Keep -e and add -ly: sincere + -ly = sincerely
3. Change -le to -ly: gentle + -ly = gently
4. Change -y to i and add -ly: happy + -ly = happily


## Exercise 2

1. The students arrive punctually every day or Every day, the students arrive punctually.
2. Her teenage daughters make breakfast quickly every day or Every day, her teenage daughters make breakfast quickly.
3. The architect didn't go to his office yesterday afternoon or Yesterday afternoon, the architect didn't go to his office.
4. She works in the library every day or Every day, she works in the library.

5. Last weekend, she drove her father to the beach or She drove her father to the beach last weekend.
6. They are planning to go to Mexico next month.


## Exercise 3

1. The driver didn't hurt his arm.
2. There was only a single passenger on the bus.
3. He didn't break it.
4. He didn't hurt any other part of his body.
5. He had only one arm.
6. He didn't hurt any other part of his body.


## Exercise 4

Even could be inserted at any slash.
1. / Margaret / offered / to clean / the oven.
2. / The boss / worked / on the weekend.
3. / During the lesson, / Jack didn't / ask a question.


## Exercise 6

1. The rules have rarely been analyzed.
2. Lying of this sort is often given the approving label of "tact."
3. A face-saving lie sometimes prevents embarrassment for the recipient.
4. Do you always tell the truth?
5. The computer displays are rarely more than a single short line in length.
6. Workers generally feel better and do a better job when they're in an attractive environment.
7. Tenants generally have more contacts with immediate neighbors than with people even a few doors away.
8. While the library was uncrowded, students almost always chose corner seats at one of the empty rectangular tables.


## Exercise 8

1. d. very hard
2. a. sometimes
3. a. never arrives
4. c. quickly
5. a. do their work very efficiently
6. b. healthy
7. a. usually arrives

CHAPTER 16: Comparisons

## Exercise 1

1. longer
2. more
3. less, fewer
4. most frequent
5. better
6. Smaller, better
7. smallest
8. cheaper, tastier
9. higher
10. better, less, faster

## Exercise 2

1. Meaning: She likes ice cream better than she likes her husband. Change to: She likes ice cream better than her husband does. (= better than her husband likes ice cream)
2. Meaning: My computer is bigger than Mary is! Change to: My computer is bigger than Mary's.
3. Meaning: I admire the president more than I admire my father. Change to: I admire the president more than my father does. (= more than my father admires the president)

## Exercise 4

Some possible answers:
1. The couch is more comfortable than the chair.
   The chair isn't as comfortable as the couch.
2. I do more work than you do.
   You do less work than I do.
   You don't do as much work as I do.
3. You speak English better than he does.
   He doesn't speak English as well as you do.
4. The governor's expertise, like the mayor's, is impressive.
   The governor's expertise is as impressive as the mayor's.
5. Sarah's dress is prettier than Jane's.
   Jane's dress isn't as pretty as Sarah's.
6. They often sleep as late as their children do.
   They, like their children, often sleep late.
7. He likes chocolate more than his wife does.
   His wife doesn't like chocolate as much as he does.
8. My father drives better than my brother.
   My brother doesn't drive as well as my father.

## Exercise 6

1. Most of the
2. Most
3. the most

32

4. Most
5. the most
6. most

## Exercise 7

1. The building is compared to a long snake. One part of the building is where the head would be.
2. The hills with the short grass are compared to a marine's head (a marine has a very short haircut).
3. Bushes and trees are compared to hair on a head; when they are removed, the shape of the head is visible.
4. The trees are compared to fence posts.
5. His hair is compared to a cloud, silver needles, and a gray mist. His eyes are compared to rocks.

## CHAPTER 17: Subject–Verb Agreement

## Exercise 1

1. develops, is
2. has, make
3. knows
4. has
5. was, accompanies
6. comes, tells, has

## Exercise 2

The four wrong verbs and their corrections are as follows:

1. Differ should be differs. The subject is way. The writer was probably misled by the word teenagers that occurs in the intervening clause modifying way: [that] teenagers act and behave.

2. Is should be are. The subject is people, which is a plural noun in English. The writer was probably thinking of the equivalent word in Spanish, which is singular.

3. Is should be are. The subject is young people in the United States. Same explanation as above.

4. Need should be needs. The subject is an old woman. The writer used the -s form with is but then neglected to use it for the second verb. Perhaps she didn't realize that every verb had to agree with its subject.

<u>Exercise</u> <u>3</u>

1. X were
2. X is
3. X shares
4. X depends
5. OK
6. X were
7. OK
8. X appear
9. X go
10. X has

<u>Exercise</u> <u>4</u>

1. My (brother) Julio <u>talks</u> to everybody, <u>asks</u> for favors, and <u>tries</u> to get
   as much as possible from people.

2. My (mother) <u>is</u> a very strict lady and (she) always <u>tries</u> to maintain
   .discipline among her children.

3. My (sister) <u>hates</u> school and <u>avoids</u> work whenever possible.

4. In my country, the (government) <u>has</u> rules and only <u>allows</u> a young couple
   to have one child.

5. The (head) of the family <u>takes</u> control and always <u>orders</u> his children to
   do jobs in the house.

<u>Exercise</u> <u>6</u>

1. are; referent of <u>which</u> is <u>traditions</u>
2. influence; referent of <u>that</u> is <u>acts</u>
3. requires; referent of <u>which</u> is <u>job</u>
4. happen; referent of <u>that</u> is <u>things</u>
5. wants; subject is <u>cousin</u>; relative clause [<u>that or whom</u>] <u>they visit</u>
   <u>every weekend</u> comes between subject and verb.
6. belongs; referent of <u>who</u> is <u>everybody</u>
7. .give; subject is <u>the relatives</u>; relative clause <u>that she lives with</u>
   comes between subject and verb.
8. influences; referent of <u>that</u> is <u>structure</u>

<u>Exercise</u> <u>8</u>

1. are
2. is
3. are
4. is

34

5. is
6. are
7. is
8. are

## Exercise 9

1. b
2. c
3. a
4. c
5. a
6. d

## Exercise 10

a. are
b. is
c. has
d. supports
e. demand
f. have to
g. are
h. are
i. are (or is)
j. have to
k. has
l. is
m. may (or might)
n. supports

## CHAPTER 18: Pronouns and Pronoun Reference

## Exercise 1

1. him and me
2. himself
3. theirs
4. you and me
5. itself
6. I , Hers, mine
7. mine
8. me

## Exercise 2

a. He
b. He
c. its
d. himself

| e. | him | m. | his |
|----|-----|----|-----|
| f. | he  | n. | his |
| g. | he  | o. | his |
| h. | his | p. | he  |
| i. | he  | q. | them |
| j. | he  | r. | his |
| k. | his | s. | his |
| l. | his | t. | we  |
|    |     | u. | he  |

## Exercise 4

1. . . . he told his uncle that . . .
2. . . . to do it.
3. . . . not having them <u>or</u> any.
4. . . . his girlfriend . . .
5. . . . its tracks . . .
6. This act <u>or</u> Her telling her parents made her brother angry. <u>Or</u> Her quitting her job made her brother angry.

## Exercise 5

| Pronoun | Referent |
|---------|----------|
| her | a farmer's daughter |
| his | the farmer |
| he | the farmer |
| he | the farmer |
| he | the farmer |
| his | the lion |
| his | the lion |
| them | teeth and claws |
| he | the lion |
| himself | the lion |
| him | the lion |
| him | the lion |

## Exercise 6

We can make a strong argument and claim that humans have to be just about the size they are in order to function as they do. In an amusing and provocative article, F. W. Went explored the impossibility of human life, as we know it, at ant dimensions. . . . Since weight increases so much faster than surface area as an object gets larger, small animals have very high ratios of surface to volume; they live in a world dominated by surface forces that affect us scarcely at all.

An ant-sized man might don some clothing, but forces of surface
adhesion would preclude its removal. The lower limit of drop size would
make showering impossible; each drop would hit with the force of a large
boulder. If our homunculus managed to get wet, and tried to dry off with a
towel, he would be stuck to it for life. He could pour no liquid, light no
fire. . . . He might pound gold leaf thin enough to construct a book for
his size, but surface adhesion would prevent the turning of pages.

## CHAPTER 19: Infinitives

### Exercise 1

| Infinitive | Function |
| --- | --- |
| to save face | Subject complement |
| to be honest | Modifying an adjective |
| to be kind | Modifying an adjective |
| to remember | Object of verb |
| to avoid | Subject complement |
| to tell | Modifying an adjective |
| to prevent | To express purpose |
| to prevent | To express purpose |
| to avoid | To express purpose |
| to achieve | Subject complement |
| to put | Modifying a noun |
| to sit around | After verb + noun phrase |
| to call | After verb + noun phrase |

### Exercise 2

1. The most frequent motive for lying was to save face.
2. The second most frequent motive for lying was to avoid conflict.
3. His dream is to send music to remote space.
4. Thomas's aim is to send science out into space.
5. The farmers' plan is to grow soybeans.
6. A designer's job is to select comfortable furniture.

### Exercise 4

We didn't wait.  She persuaded us to leave.
She tried to persuade us to wait, but she failed.  We left.

Her advice was that they should arrive on time.
Her students were all late. It wasn't her fault. She didn't tell them to arrive late.


## Exercise 6

1. It is difficult to fix a broken window.
2. He is difficult to understand.
3. It is hard for me to understand trigonometry.
4. I find it hard to understand algebra, too.
5. It is easy to please our teacher.
6. That jar is difficult to open.
7. It is hard to learn the new word processing program.
8. The boss is easy for most employees to get along with.
9. A manual typewriter is difficult to use after an electric one.
10. Statistical methods are hard to learn.


## Exercise 10

1. to be told
2. to be fooled
3. to have been invited
4. to have had
5. to be noticed
6. to have survived
7. to be admitted
8. to have recovered


## CHAPTER 20: –ing Forms (Gerunds and Modifiers)

## Exercise 1

| Verbal | Function |
|--------|----------|
| bursting | Clause substitute: adverbial |
| seeing | Object of preposition |
| stumbling | Subject |
| hiding | Noun modifying noun |
| seeing | Object of preposition |


## Exercise 4

1. living
2. to drink
3. drinking
4. driving
5. drive
6. lying

7. to go
8. going
9. taking
10. to be


## Exercise 6

1. to send, explaining
2. buying, trying, to buy, sitting, to test
3. to send, not to touch
4. to discourage, spending, to move
5. to know, informing, destroying
6. having to, deceiving


# CHAPTER 21: Participle Forms (-ed/-en Forms)

## Exercise 1

| Participle | Function |
|---|---|
| 1. prepared | Clause substitute (adjectival) |
| 2. domesticated | Adjective |
| 3. depleted | Clause substitute (adjectival) |
| 4. valued | Adjective after linking verb |
| 5. associated | Clause substitute (adjectival) |
| 6. developed | Adjective |

## Exercise 2

1. sprawling
2. lashed
3. delighted
4. concealing
5. excited
6. smoked, stewed

## Exercise 3

Possible answers:
1. a. The loud radio annoyed Julie.
   b. Julie found the loud radio annoying.
   c. Julie was annoyed by the sound of the loud radio.
2. a. The lecture confused the students.
   b. The lecture was confusing for the students.
   c. The students were confused by the lecture.
3. a. The end of the movie surprised us.
   b. We thought the end of the movie was surprising.
   c. We were surprised by the end of the movie.

4. a. The exam results disappointed the students.
   b. The exam results were disappointing to the students.
   c. The students were disappointed by the exam results.
5. a. The big dog frightened the little girl.
   b. The little girl found the big dog frightening.
   c. The little girl was frightened by the big dog.
6. a. The meal satisfied the diners.
   b. The diners found the meal very satisfying.
   c. The diners were satisfied with the meal.

## Exercise 5

1. leaving
2. leave
3. jumping
4. reprimand
5. seeing
6. driving

## Exercise 7

| Participle | Line | Function |
|---|---|---|
| recognized | 13 | Part of passive verb |
| produced | 14 | Adjectival clause substitute |
| sold | 14 | Part of passive verb |
| sold | 17 | Part of passive verb (infinitive) |
| produced | 19 | Adjectival clause substitute |
| sold | 20 | Part of passive verb |
| intended | 21 | Part of passive verb |
| exported | 22 | Part of passive verb (infinitive) |
| consumed | 22 | Part of passive verb (infinitive) |
| noted | 23 | Adverbial clause substitute |
| exported | 27 | Part of passive verb |

## Exercise 8

1. c
2. b
3. a
4. b
5. c
6. a
7. b
8. d

# CHAPTER 22: Coordinating Conjunctions

## Exercise 1

Note that on some occasions and and other coordinating conjunctions do not connect complete sentences, each with its own subject and verb: I found a niche . . . and started drawing . . .(connects two verbs); I laughed, saying that it was only a drawing and [that] I would be happy if he would take it (connects two noun clauses introduced by that).

| Line | Conjunction |
|------|-------------|
| 76 | but |
| 77 | and |
| 80 | and |
| 83 | and |
| 89 | and |
| 91 | and |
| 93 | and |
| 97 | and |
| 98 | so |
| 111 | for |
| 113 | but |
| 114 | and |
| 116 | so |
| 117 | but |
| 119 | but |
| 122 | or |
| 125 | and |

## Exercise 2

1. The two brothers are playing happily with their own toys, and although minutes have passed, neither has made a grab for the other's toy.
2. The younger one is babbling to himself in pidgin English, and the older one is singing ceaselessly.
3. His baby can't catch him yet, but it's only a matter of time.
4. My brother interested my girl friends, and I was interested in his boy friends.
5. He was about to say hello, but what came out instead was "You can't catch me."

## Exercise 3

1. CS
2. OK
3. RO
4. CS
5. CS
6. OK

41

## Exercise 4

1. I have vivid memories of reading in a club chair and having my brother enter the room.
2. One night your husband comes home and tells you that he has decided to have a second wife.
3. She will be younger and cuter than you.
4. My younger brother turned into a good-looking teenage boy and a first-rate dancer.
5. He has no interest in the trucks or the sandbox.

## Exercise 6

1. He doesn't earn a lot, nor has he saved any money.
2. She isn't working hard, nor is she trying hard or She is neither working hard nor trying hard.
3. She can't type, nor does she want to learn.
4. He won't take his father's advice, nor will he listen to his best friends or He will neither take his father's advice nor listen to his best friends.
5. At this time, inflation can't be stopped, nor can it be reduced or At this time, inflation can be neither stopped nor reduced.

## Exercise 7

1. She doesn't use her living room, and neither do I.
2. She wanted a pool, and so did I.
3. She had a color scheme, and her friend did too.
4. She doesn't like phones in living rooms, and her sister doesn't either.
5. She doesn't want a TV set in the living room, and neither do her children.
6. She worked in the bedroom, and so did her daughter.

## Exercise 8

And occurs four times. The first three times it connects two sentences; the fourth time it connects two verbs.

## CHAPTER 23: Transitions

## Exercise 2

The underlined transition word is the one the author used, in its original position. The slash mark (/) shows the other places where that transition (or another) could occur.

1. / Our friend, however, persisted / .

2. <u>Similarly</u>, most of the steel produced in Pittsburgh, Pennsylvania, and Gary, Indiana, is / sold outside those cities.
3. / The basic industry <u>thus</u> supports 400 people.
4. <u>That is</u>, for every miner employed in the town's basic industry, / three people may be employed in a nonbasic industry.
5. / You might, <u>for example</u>, cover up your mistakes by blaming them on outside forces / .
6. / You might, <u>for example</u>, compliment a friend's bad work / . . .
7. <u>Likewise</u>, you might / hide feelings of irritation to avoid a fight.
8. / You might, <u>for instance</u>, pretend / to be glad to see someone you actually dislike.
9. <u>On the other hand</u>, if the goal / is to keep customers in a bar or restaurant for a long time / . . .
10. <u>For example</u>, Sommer / watched students in a college library / and found . . .

## Exercise 4

The sentences can be treated as two sentences or combined as one separated by a semicolon. Only one of the alternatives is shown, though either would be acceptable.

1. CS; however,
2. CS; Still,
3. RO; for instance,
4. CS; for example,
5. OK
6. RO; Then

## Exercise 5

1. however, nevertheless, still, nonetheless
2. however, nevertheless, still, nonetheless
3. however, on the other hand, in contrast
4. However, Nevertheless, Still, Nonetheless
5. However, On the other hand, In contrast
6. on the contrary, rather
7. On the contrary, Rather
8. however, though

## CHAPTER 24: Adjectival Clauses

## Exercise 3

1. The girl who is sitting in the front row asks a lot of questions.
2. I'm really annoyed with the girl that (<u>or</u> who) asks a lot of questions.
3. Pass me the books that are lying on the table.
4. I paid the boy who (<u>or</u> that) delivered the groceries.
5. I wrote a review of the book that impressed me so much.

6. The results teach a lesson that isn't surprising.
7. The journalist who wants to interview you at noon tomorrow works for a newsmagazine.
8. She applied for the job that was advertised in the daily newspaper.


## Exercise 4

1. The environment [that] the architects have created can communicate discomfort.
2. The people [that] I met at a party last night are from California.
3. I want the TV [that] I saw in the store window yesterday.
4. There's the house [that] I like.
5. The couch [that] I want to buy has a high back.
6. I know the furniture store [that] you want to visit.
7. The seating arrangement [that] the architect designed was pleasant.
8. The kitchen cabinets [that] the architect designed were too high.


## Exercise 5

1. The neighbor whose window I broke . . .
2. The man whose daughter I met last night . . .
3. The novel whose beginning [or the beginning of which] I read last week . . .
4. The school whose curriculum was praised in the newspaper recently . . .
5. The person whose views I respect a great deal . . .
6. The doctor whose patient died yesterday . . .


## Exercise 8

The following need commas:

2. Theo, who worked in an art-dealer's shop, introduced . . .
9. . . . the oldest member of the family, who opened his eyes . . .
10. . . . an "ugly" one, which resembled . . .


## Exercise 9

1. . . . people, most of whom . . .
2. . . . members, most of whom . . .
3. . . . songs, one of which . . .
4. . . . cakes, neither of which . . .
5. . . . brothers, one of whom . . .
6. . . . poems, many of which . . .


## Exercise 10

1. . . . a house overlooking . . .
2. The chairs standing in a row . . .
3. The people applauding that comedian . . .
4. He is the one trying to get on TV.
5. The jokes told at the party . . .

6. Any performer not offering to go . . .
7. The prize awarded at the ceremony . . .


## CHAPTER 25: Noun Clauses and Reported Speech

### Exercise 5

1. . . . what his name is.
2. . . . why he stands so close.
3. . . . when he will arrive.
4. . . . when she was born.
5. . . . what the ambassador wants.
6. . . . how long he has been waiting.
7. . . . why he got so angry.
8. . . . whose report that is.
9. . . . what the square root of 1369 is.
10. . . . why you are staring at me.
11. . . . why you arrived so early.
12. . . . if it is going to be good weather next month? (The introductory phrase is a question: How do I know . . . ?)
13. . . . if a Scotsman wears anything under his kilt.
14. . . . if the French won the Battle of Waterloo.

### Exercise 6

One version follows. Others are possible.
. . . Teacher Wu asked him if his mother was a pianist. He told her that she had once been a pianist but that she now played the harpsichord. Teacher Wu wondered if he knew what a piano should sound like, since he had grown up hearing it every day. He thought he did.

### Exercise 7

1. . . . a decision: "We will give you one of the rowboats."
2. I looked at Old Ding and said, "That is absolutely ridiculous. I won't take a boat from your family in return for a charcoal sketch."
3. They told me, "Please, by all means, speak up."
4. They said, "Of course you can have whatever you want."
5. The family said, "Your decision has true spirit."

Exercise 4

1. They are so rich that they can afford . . .
2. He had such a good time canoeing in Canada that he decided . . .
3. She has such a lot of free time that she has offered . . .
4. He has so many books that he doesn't know where . . .
5. This book is so interesting that I think I'll . . .
6. This is such an interesting book that I think I'll . . .
7. She ran so quickly that I couldn't . . .
8. He traded in his car so that he could buy . . .
9. She went to bed early so that she would be alert . . .
10. The economists made a conservative estimate so that they would not be accused . . .


Exercise 5

Possible answers:
1. Even though China had been the major supplier of soybeans to the world market, the course of postwar politics . . .
2. Though his baby can't catch him yet, it's only . . .
3. Although I haven't had much time to practice it since then, nowadays I try . . .
4. In spite of the fact that my mother played the piano, I had never learned . . .
5. Although I had walked along the river many times since meeting the fisherman that day in winter, I did not see . . .
6. Though most people would agree that lying to gain advantage over an unknowing subject is wrong, another kind of mistruth . . .


Exercise 6

1. He fixed the piano before eating dinner.
2. She thanked him after trying it out.
3. While working, he listened to music.
4. He listened to Michael Jackson (in order) to set middle C.
5. Feeling grateful, she made him a wonderful dinner.
6. Before leaving, he thanked her for the meal.


Exercise 7

1. . . . I refused to wear it because I thought . . .
2. . . . from the city because they have . . .
3. . . . and has more fresh air, it's still . . .
4. . . . more time to study because they save . . .
5. . . . grown-up people, he doesn't enjoy . . .
6. . . . on children because young children . . .

1. b
2. a
3. d
4. c
5. b


## CHAPTER 27: Adverbial Clauses: Conditions

### Exercise 3

1. If the sun were shining today, we would [or we'd] play tennis.
2. If Lucy were in school today, she could bring your book home with her.
3. If I had a car, you could borrow it.
4. If she were a conscientious student, she would get high grades.
5. If the teacher were here, the class would begin.
6. If I had some money, you could borrow $20 from me.
7. If I were living in England, I'd [or I would] live in a thatched cottage.
8. If it weren't snowing now, we'd [or we would] walk to town.
9. If the price went down [or were to go down], I would [or I'd] buy that VCR.
10. If my grandfather were alive, he'd [or he would] enjoy this view.

### Exercise 5

| Meaning | if or unless Clause | Independent Clause |
|---|---|---|
| Hindsight | had been told | would have had |
| Hindsight | had been taught | would have been |


## CHAPTER 28: Style

### Exercise 1

Possible answers:
1. Parents and children should discuss sex education.
2. Parents should recognize the generation gap.
3. The Senate and the House of Representatives establish the laws in the United States.
4. The four boys in my family fight a lot.
5. A few people I know refused to continue their studies.

## Exercise 3

1. . . . The bean was tested and it met the need perfectly.
2. . . . They were introduced to the New World by Samuel Bowen.
3. . . . After each table was occupied by one reader, new readers . . .
4. . . . The most detailed study was probably conducted by Raymond Adams and Bruce Biddle.


## CHAPTER 29: Punctuation


## Exercise 1

1. F
2. F
3. F
4. F
5  F
6. CS
7. F
8.  RO


## Exercise 2

One possibility:
    According to Brueghel, when Icarus fell, it was spring.  A farmer was ploughing his field.  The whole pageantry of the year was awake, tingling near the edge of the sea, concerned with itself, sweating in the sun that melted the wings' wax. Unsignificantly, off the coast, there was a splash, quite unnoticed. This was Icarus drowning.


## Exercise 3

The original passage looks like this:
    In the early 1960s, the first minicomputers were made commercially. They were the size of a two-drawer file cabinet.  The revolution was on. Less than a decade later, the microcomputer was invented.  The basic unit of the microcomputer is a tiny silicon chip less than 1 cm on a side.  Each chip is a miniature electronic circuit that serves the different computer functions.  Amazingly, each circuit contains thousands of elements.


## Exercise 4

a.  5.  To separate clauses
b.  3.  Around inserted material
c.  2.  Between items in a list
d.  2.  Between items in a list
e.  5.  To separate clauses
f.  3.  Around inserted material

g.  3.  Around inserted material
n.  3.  Around inserted material
i.  4.  Before a quotation
j.  3.  Around inserted material
k.  5   To separate dependent clauses
l.  1.  Before the subject
m.  3.  Around inserted material

## Exercise 5

The original passages are punctuated as follows:
1. The 400 people demand services: schools and churches have to be built,
   grocery and clothing stores and livery stables are operated, newspapers
   are published, professional personnel are needed, and saloons have to
   cater to visiting cowboys.
2. On the national level, if a society chooses to go to war, it must give
   up some consumer goods.
3. In the winter of 1888, while Seurat was attracting attention in Paris
   and Cézanne was working in his seclusion in Aix, a young earnest
   Dutchman left Paris for southern France in search of the intense light
   and color of the south. He was Vincent van Gogh. Van Gogh was born in
   Holland in 1853, the son of a vicar.
4. In the smallest of the portable computers, the cathode ray tube has
   been replaced by a flat electroluminescent display and the disk drives
   by bubble memory chips. In these computers, information is stored on
   the road, in the classroom, at conferences, at the library, or
   elsewhere.
5. On a hot June afternoon I met the lab's director, John McCarthy. . . .
   McCarthy's appearance, when he finally strode into the office, struck
   me as extraordinary. He is about average height, five feet nine
   inches. His build is average, with a little age trying to collect
   itself around his middle.

## Exercise 7

1. The child's toys are all over the floor.
2. Her children's dolls are lying all over the floor.
3. The director's plans will be put into operation.
4. The politicians' plans might be delayed.
5. The women's plans are being attacked.

## Exercise 8

1. C: That is
2. C: How is
3. P
4. P
5. P
6. C: I am; C: It has

<u>Exercise 9</u>

Possible answers:
She said, "I grew up playing, and I continued to study when I was in America. I bought the piano in America and brought it back to China when I returned with my husband."

She said to me, "Will you play a duet with me?"

I said, "I wish I could help you. But even though my mother played the piano, I have never learned how to tune or repair one."

I said to her, "Please don't stay in the apartment while I work, because it will only make me more nervous."

She promised, "You'll have a good dinner this evening."

I stood up and said, "You're very welcome. But I have work to do now and should be getting back."

She pleaded with me, "Please stay. Have some tea and candies with me, please."


<u>Exercise 10</u>

The original punctuation is given here. Variations may be acceptable.

Although most people would agree that lying to gain advantage over an unknowing subject is wrong, another kind of mistruth—the "white lie"—is both a popular and often acceptable type of communication. White lies are defined (at least by those who tell them) as being unmalicious, or even helpful.

Whether or not they are benign, white lies are certainly common. In one study, . . . 130 subjects were asked to keep track of the truthfulness of their everyday conversational statements. Only 38.5 percent of these statements—slightly more than a third—proved to be totally honest. What reasons do people give for being deceitful so often? . . .

When subjects in the study . . . were asked to give a lie-by-lie account of their motives for concealing or distorting the truth, five major reasons emerged. The most frequent motive (occurring in 55.2 percent of the lies) was <u>to save face</u>. Lying of this sort is often given the approving label of "tact," and is used "when it would be unkind to be honest but dishonest to be kind" (Bavelas, 1983). Sometimes a face-saving lie prevents embarrassment for the recipient, as when you pretend to remember someone at a party whom you really don't recall ever having seen before. In other cases a lie protects the teller from embarrassment. You might, for example, cover up your mistakes by blaming them on outside forces: "You didn't receive the check? It must have been delayed in the mail."

PART II: ADDITIONAL EXERCISES FOR THE READINGS

This section includes additional exercises for each reading. If you organize your course around the readings and their writing assignments, turning to the grammar chapters for review and for teaching new structures, you might find these additional sections useful.

The preview questions can be discussed before your students do the reading. You might want to take a few minutes for this at the end of a class; the students could then do the reading at home. Then, in the next class, you could discuss some of the response questions and the questions for analysis before the students begin to discuss their ideas for one of the writing assignments attached to the readings. The students can write the essay at home, and from that draft you can see which grammar points they find troublesome. At this point, whole-class instruction, group work, individual conferences, or individual assignments can be built around the grammar chapters. At the end of each reading, the grammar chapters in which excerpts from the reading are used for examples or exercises are listed.


ROOM WITH VIEW—AND NO PEOPLE: Nora Ephron

Nora Ephron is a journalist, novelist, and film scriptwriter. She has written frequently for The New York Post and The New York Times.


Preview Questions

1. Do you know any people who have a room in their house or apartment that is hardly ever used? Which room is that, and why is it not used much?

2. What is the most-used room in your house? Why is it used the most?

3. Do you have a living room in your house? If so, when and how is it used?


Response Questions

1. What were the first thoughts you had as you finished reading the article? What connections or associations does the article lead you to make with your own experience?

2. Would an article like this be likely to appear in a magazine in your country or any other country you know? Or does the author's viewpoint seem confined to the culture of North America?

3. What do you infer about Nora Ephron (about her age, personality, views, tastes, lifestyle, etc.) from this article? Do you know anyone like her?

## Analysis

1. Look closely at the first paragraph of Ephron's article. Is it composed mostly of long or short sentences? Is the paragraph an effective lead-in to the subject for you, the reader?

2. Most of the article is about Ephron, her home, her actions, and her views. In paragraph five, she tells the story of Lillian. Why do you think she tells this story in the article?

3. The author makes the point about not using the living room early in the article, in the first paragraph. How does the author conclude the article and how does that conclusion relate to the point that no one uses the living room?

4. Which words occur in the first sentence of every paragraph? What effect does the repetition have? Did you notice it the first time you read the article?

5. The article was written by a journalist for a Sunday newspaper magazine to entertain rather than inform the readers. The writer uses an informal, conversational tone to make the article light and accessible; she uses sencence structure and expressions that would not be common in more formal academic writing. What examples of informal and conversational usage can you find?

## THE DOCTORS' DILEMMA: Sissela Bok

Sissela Bok has taught medical ethics at Harvard Medical School and at Brandeis University, Massachusetts, and is the author of Lying: Moral Choices in Public and Private Life (1978) and Secrets: On the Ethics of Concealment and Revelation (1982).

## Preview Questions

1. Do you think that professionals—lawyers, doctors, teachers, politicians, business people—have an obligation always to tell the truth? Or is deception ever justified? What makes you think the way you do on this issue?

2. Is there a saying in your language similar to "What you don't know can't hurt you"? Is it ever applied as an ethical principle in public life?

3. Which people do you know or have you read about who have been faced with a dilemma about whether to be honest or not?

## Response Questions

1. After you read the second paragraph, what was your immediate reaction to

the situation described there? Did you answer, "Yes, they should conceal the truth," or "No, they should not conceal the truth"?

2. What connections or associations does the article lead you to make with your experience or with your reading?

3. What is Bok's point of view on the issue of whether doctors should lie to patients or not? What specific sentences state that point of view? Do you agree with her point of view? Why or why not?

## Analysis

1. What type of sentence does the writer use to introduce us to the subject? What type of sentence does she use for every sentence in paragraph two? Why do you think she chooses this device?

2. The article is written predominantly in one time framework (present-future). Only at one point does the writer move out of that framework into the past. Where does that occur, and why?

3. The author begins by giving us information about why doctors feel it is acceptable to lie. Then the article reaches a turning point, and Bok emphasizes the benefits of telling the truth. Where do you think that turning point occurs? What word signals it?

4. Bok mentions arguments on both sides of the issue of whether doctors should lie to benefit their patients or not. Write down briefly the arguments she gives on each side.

## THE SOYBEAN: Fred Hapgood

Fred Hapgood is a journalist who often writes about connections between science and ordinary life. He lives in Boston.

## Preview Questions

1. Which crops are grown in your country, and how important are they for the economy of your country?

2. What are the staple foods eaten in your country (for example, bread, rice, corn, potatoes)?

3. What food do you like to eat? Is that food good for you nutritionally?

4. Have you ever eaten tofu (doufu)? If so, how was it prepared and served?

## Response Questions

1. The soybean is rich in protein. What other foods are a good source of protein?

2. How are the following cultivated: rice, wheat, corn, coffee, bananas?

3. Which of the soybean's three virtues would you consider the most important?

4. In paragraph five, we read of some sayings associated with doufu. Are there sayings in your language that make associations with items of food? What are they? In the United States, people refer to someone who is a bit crazy as "nutty as a fruitcake." And people and things can be called "as American as apple pie." In Australia, a saying is "Don't come the raw prawn with me!"

5. In paragraph seven, we read about how the Japanese imported aspects of Chinese culture. Which aspects of other cultures has your country imported?

## Analysis

1. In the first paragraph of this excerpt, which elements does the writer introduce? Are these elements explained and expanded later in the article? If so, where?

2. Notice that the pronoun "I" occurs in the second paragraph. The author then does not mention "I" again until paragraph five. What was the purpose of introducing himself in paragraph two? He could, after all, have omitted the first part of the first sentence and just continued the narrative account he began in the first paragraph.

3. What is the focus of the first four paragraphs? That is, what do they tell us about?

4. Paragraphs five and six appear to interrupt the historical account. Would you prefer to read the article without those two paragraphs? Why or why not?

THE SURPRISE: Russell Baker

Russell Baker is a journalist. He writes a regular column for The New York Times. His two autobiographical volumes (Growing Up and The Good Times) describe his boyhood and adolescence in the Depression and his early years as a journalist. This excerpt appeared untitled in Growing Up.

## Preview Questions

1. What are your family's rituals for giving presents to one another?

2. Have you ever discovered a secret that you shouldn't have discovered? What was it, and what happened?

3. Have you ever planned a surprise for someone that didn't work out as you had planned? What happened?

## Response Questions

1. As you read the excerpt, who did you identify with more: Russell Baker or his mother? Why?

2. Do you think Russell Baker did right to conceal from his mother that he knew of her surprise? Or should he have been frank and told the truth immediately?

3. Baker had wanted a bicycle very much. What objects have you desperately wanted to own? Did you get them?

4. What surprises have members of your family planned for each other?

## Analysis

1. This excerpt is divided into three paragraphs. What do you think determines the boundaries of the paragraphs; that is, what is the focus of each one? Would any other division work as well for you, the reader?

2. In one place the author has deliberately used a sentence fragment. Where? Can you speculate as to why he chose not to write a complete sentence?

3. How would the sentences in the reading passage change if you had to continue them as follows:

      Line 5:  She kept the door locked, but I needed . . .
      Line 12: I was overwhelmed when I . . .
      Line 15: Still, when I stumbled . . .
      Line 19: I resolved that I must do nothing to reveal what I . . .

4. Retell the incident from the point of view of Russell Baker's mother. Now she will be the "I" of the story, and you will tell the incident from her perspective.

VINCENT VAN GOGH: E.H. Gombrich

E.H. Gombrich is an art historian, who has taught at universities in
England (note the British spelling, <u>colour</u>, in the excerpt) and the United
States. <u>The Story of Art</u>, first published in 1950 but with many later
editions, is his best-known book.


## Preview Questions

1. Who are the most famous artists in your country and what kind of work do
they do? Do you know anything about the artists' lives?

2. If you could have any painting by any artist to hang on your wall at
home, which painting would you choose, and why?

3. The common image of artists is that most of them live in garrets and
have a hard time making a living, with only very few making enough money to
be able to live from their art. Do you think that society should provide
more support for artists? If so, what kind of support?


## Response Questions

1. The passage mentions artists Seurat, Cézanne, Millet, and Raphael as
well as Vincent van Gogh. Use an encyclopedia or art history books to find
reproductions of some paintings by these artists.

2. Who are the famous artists in your country? Tell the other students in
the class about their work.

3. From reading this piece about Vincent van Gogh, what would you expect a
painting of his room in Arles to look like? Discuss this; then turn to
page 6 to see the painting.


## Analysis

1. This one long paragraph tells us briefly about Vincent van Gogh's life.
Examine how the paragraph is organized: is it organized exactly according
to chronological time? If not, what devices are used?

2. This passage is an excerpt from a book called <u>The Story of Art</u>. What
do you imagine the function of the opening sentence of this paragraph to
be? What do you think preceded this paragraph?

3. The pattern of the first sentence is this:

In ⁓⁓⁓(time), while ⁓⁓⁓⁓⁓⁓⁓⁓, subject + verb

Make up a few sentences using this pattern that tell about your own
experience.

4. A good way to learn new vocabulary is to learn word forms as you come
across a new word. Keep a chart like the one below:

| Adjective | Noun | Verb | Adverb |
|-----------|------|------|--------|
| attractive | attraction | attract | attractively |

Which word forms can you derive from the following words that appear in the passage: earnest, religious, impress, decide, introduce, ungrudgingly, finance? Fill them in on a chart like the one above.

## SIBLINGS: Anna Quindlen

Anna Quindlen is a journalist who for many years wrote a nationally syndicated column. She lives in New York City and is married with three children. This article originally appeared without a title as a column in the series "Life in the 30s" in The New York Times.

## Preview Questions

1. If you have any brothers or sisters, how would you characterize your relationship with them? Is it one of friendship or resentment?

2. What incidents have you participated in or witnessed that illustrate sibling rivalry?

3. What do you think is the ideal number of children in a family? Why?

## Response Questions

1. What stories can you remember from your own childhood that illustrate your relationship with your brothers and sisters?

2. Who do your sympathies lie with the most: the author, Quin (the older son), or Christopher (the younger son)? Why?

3. Think of families that you know: is the dominant sibling relationship one of friendship or resentment? Give an example.

4. What incidents in your own life do you think of as you read the article?

## Analysis

1. What point of view is Quindlen expressing about the subject of "siblings"? At what point in the article does she most explicitly state that point of view?

2. She supports her point of view with stories—that is, with incidents and examples from her own childhood and from her own children's experiences. Make a summary list of the stories she uses.

3. Which paragraph presents a kind of turning point, offering a new point of view about siblings in contrast to the one already presented?

4. In the fifth paragraph, Quindlen compares the arrival of a new sibling to the arrival of a new wife. How effective is that analogy? What other analogies would be possible?

## CULTURAL EXCHANGES: Mark Salzman

Mark Salzman taught English and studied martial arts in China for two years. Iron and Silk is an account of his adventures. The two excerpts included are from different chapters of the book. The title has been added.

### Preview Questions

1. What kind of meal is a real luxury in your country?

2. What are the rituals in your country when a guest is about to leave your house? (For example, what does the host do and say, how is the guest expected to respond, etc.?)

3. What is the custom in your country when someone gives a gift? How is it accepted? When is it opened? Is a gift made in return?

4. What is the attitude toward "talking straight" (talking frankly) in your country?

### Response Questions

1. Without looking at the two excerpts again, tell in a sentence or two what you particularly noted as you read: what parts did you like or have personal connections with?

2. Did the telling of the stories make you think of any events in your life or in the life of someone you know? Tell those stories.

3. Can you play any musical instruments? Have you ever drawn pictures? Have you ever exchanged your work for something else? Tell about this.

4. The author mentions a superstition. What superstitions affect human relationships in your culture?

5. Do you think that the conversations between Mark Salzman and the Chinese people he met took place in Chinese or in English? What makes you think that?

6. How do you think Mark Salzman felt when the family offered to give him a rowboat?

## Analysis

1. In the first paragraph of the first "exchange," why do you think Salzman included the details about Teacher Wu's apartment? Why do you think he included facts like the "bare cement walls" and the "bare light bulb"?

2. What few words could you write to capture what the third paragraph of the first "exchange" is about?

3. If paragraph 18 went like this:
    We had a delicious meal. Then Teacher Wu sat down at the piano . . .
    etc.
how would that make a difference for the reader?

4. The second "exchange" is told in two paragraphs. What is the link between the two paragraphs? What new point does the second paragraph take up?


**THE EFFECTS OF OUR ENVIRONMENT: Ronald B. Adler, Lawrence B. Rosenfeld, and Neil Towne**

This excerpt is from the third edition of Interplay: The Process of Interpersonal Communication, a textbook used in college courses.

## Preview Questions

1. Which buildings or rooms make you feel good to be in them? What are the special features that contribute to the feeling of pleasure?

2. Have you ever been in places that made you feel particularly comfortable or uncomfortable? What were they like?

3. How would you react if you were in a fairly empty library and someone chose to sit right next to you or directly opposite you?

4. If you were going to buy a couch, an armchair, and a desk, what features would you look for in each?

## Response Questions

1. Reflect on the homes you have visited lately and whether they were places where you could relax. Describe some of them to students in your class.

2. What experiences have you had of work space affecting the effectiveness of your work and your attitude toward it?

3. What kind of environment do you like in a restaurant (big, crowded, bustling, and noisy—or small, intimate, peaceful, and quiet)?

4. Tell about a pleasant or unpleasant time at an airport, in a restaurant or bar, in a doctor's office, or in a library, when the feelings you had were attributable to the design of the space.

5. Look around at the classroom you are in: what features of its design and furnishings could be improved?


## Analysis

1. The authors present an unfamiliar concept of "unliving rooms." How do they explain to us what that concept means?

2. Look closely at paragraph two. The paragraph begins and ends by using verbs in the present time cluster; the middle portion of the paragraph uses past time verbs. How would you explain the decisions to make the switches? Would there be any other way of organizing the paragraph?

3. In paragraph four, the authors include a sentence in parentheses. Why do you think they put that sentence within parentheses?

4. In paragraph two, what tense is used in the sentences following "Maslow and Mintz found that . . ."? In paragraph five, which tense is used in the sentences following "Sommer also describes how . . ."? In paragraph seven, which tense is used following "Sommer found that . . ."? What comments can you make about those choices?

5. In paragraph eight, which one sentence more than any other expresses the main idea of the paragraph? (That is, which sentence could be seen as the topic sentence of the paragraph?)

6. The last three paragraphs are devoted to discussion of one idea. How could you express it in just a few words?

7. Make an outline of the passage, grouping the twelve paragraphs into blocks according to the points they make.


## TAU CETI: Lewis Thomas

Lewis Thomas is a physician, educator, and science writer. His best known books are Lives of a Cell and Medusa and the Snail.


## Preview Questions

1. What do you think are the greatest achievements of mankind? What would you like to send to another planet to show its inhabitants what mankind has done? If you had to send something representative of your country and culture, what would you send?

2. Do you ever look up at the stars? If you do, what do you think about?

3. What five questions would you like to send off into space to ask the inhabitants of another planet?

## Response Questions

1. How many alternatives does Thomas propose for sending news of our civilization into space? Which one would you favor, and why?

2. If you wanted to leave a personal memento of yourself for your great-great-great grandchildren, something that would convey to them what kind of person you are, what would you leave, and why?

3. Some researchers talk about freezing human beings' bodies and waking them up a hundred years later. Under what circumstances would that be acceptable to you?

4. If you wanted to send to another planet something that showed twentieth century life at its worst, what would you send, and why?

6. Thomas mentions telling "the harder truths later." What do you think he means by that?

7. Thomas fears that 200 years from now our science and technology will have advanced so much that our present-day technology will not be at all impressive. Speculate about what might be possible 200 years from now.

## Analysis

1. What is the topic of paragraph four—that is, what is it about? Write a one-word summary. Do the same for paragraphs five and six.

2. Reread Thomas's concluding sentence to his chapter on Tau Ceti. What does he do in this paragraph? (Does he, for example, summarize his previous points, or use a quotation? If not, how does he end his chapter?)

3. In paragraph one, Thomas imagines a short dialogue: "Hello are you there?" "Yes, hello." Then, in the final paragraph, he quotes the same lines again. Why do you think he does that? What effect does it have on you, the reader?

4. In paragraph six, Thomas mentions questions and then lists six possibilities. He then says, "There is no end to this list." Why do you think he only listed six questions? Why not many more? Or why not just one?

**PORTABLE COMPUTERS: Alexander Taffel**

This excerpt is taken from the fifth edition of a high school textbook called <u>Physics: Its Methods and Meanings</u>.

## Preview Questions

1. Have you used a computer? What have you used it for?

2. Do you think it is necessary for people to learn how to program computers? Why or why not?

3. What have been the good and bad points of computers and programs you have used?

4. What kinds of tasks can computers do well, and in what areas of business do you think they will have the most impact? What do you think their impact on education will be?

## Response Questions

1. What other examples do you know of objects that illustrate the principle "Smaller is better"?

2. What technological developments, inventions, and improvements have you seen in your lifetime?

3. What do you expect will happen with computer technology in the future?

4. If you could have a telephone attached to a video screen with a picture of the person calling you, would you want that? Why or why not?

## Analysis

1. The excerpt contains six paragraphs. Read it a paragraph at a time. After you have read each paragraph, close the book and write one or two sentences of your own to summarize what the paragraph says.

2. Researchers are working on developing computers that can read handwritten words. If you wanted to include information on those computers, where in this passage would you include it?

3. In the third paragraph, the words bubble memory appear three times. How could you rewrite the paragraph so that you you do not use that term so many times?

4. What brief headings could you write to indicate the focus of paragraphs two, three, and four? Paragraph one, for example, could be headed From Big to Little.

# ARTIFICIAL INTELLIGENCE: Philip J.Hilts

Philip J. Hilts is a reporter and free-lance writer who specializes in science writing. He has published frequently in The Washington Post, Omni, and Science.

## Preview Questions

1. What advances in technology have you seen in your lifetime and what do you expect to see?

2. What do you think are the most important effects that the development of robots could have on society?

3. In what ways have you seen computers used or used computers yourself? How would the activity have been done without computers?

## Response Questions

1. What do you know about artificial intelligence?

2. What do you see as promising things that computers might be able to do one day?

3. Some people play chess against a computer program. What are the advantages and disadvantages of playing against a program rather than another human being?

4. If you could have a robot of your own, what would you want to have it programmed to do?

## Analysis

1. In which of the seven paragraphs of this reading passage do we learn the most about John McCarthy as a person?

2. Where do those paragraphs occur in the reading? What information interrupts the information about McCarthy?

3. Details about McCarthy occur throughout the passage. Make one list of what you learn about his physical appearance and another list about his work and work habits.

4. The author of this passage chose to write about not only trends in contemporary science but also the scientists themselves as people. Does this approach appeal to your interests?

## THE CULTURE OF "LEAD TIME": Edward T. Hall

Edward T. Hall is an anthropologist who has written books examining the concepts of space and time and cultural differences. This excerpt is from The Silent Language, originally published in 1959.


### Preview Questions

1. If you invited people to come to your home for a social gathering at 7.30 P.M., what time would you expect guests to arrive?

2. In your country, if someone makes an appointment to see a business person or official, say at 2 P.M., at what time would that person start to feel uncomfortable and angry if he were kept waiting?

3. Have you ever been kept waiting for a long time? How did you feel? How did you react?


### Response Questions

1. How would you have reacted if you were the business colleague who was kept waiting?

2. The passage discusses differences in the concept of "lead time" between the United States and other countries. What cultural rules in your country might cause problems for visitors from abroad?

3. Do you think that the minister shared the blame for the misunderstanding—or was it all the fault of the foreign visitor?

4. What are the principal sources of misunderstanding between officials in your country and foreign visitors? How could these misunderstandings be prevented?


### Analysis

1. The sentence in line 29: "The attaché's stay in the country was not a happy one" tells us a great deal. Why do you think it wasn't happy, and in what ways wasn't it happy?

2. "Cooling one's heels" is an idiomatic expression. How would such a concept of passing time while waiting for something important to happen be expressed in your language?

3. Most of this excerpt tells a story about an American in a Latin country What point is Hall illustrating with this story? What concept does this story provide the reader evidence of?

4. Hall is presenting a contrast between American and Latin customs. He uses a lot of words and phrases that indicate contrast. However is one such word. What other expressions of contrast does Hall use?

**SIZING UP HUMAN INTELLIGENCE:** Stephen Jay Gould

Stephen Jay Gould is a paleontologist and educator. He has taught at
Harvard University for many years. This excerpt is taken from his book
Ever since Darwin: Reflections on Natural History, published in 1977.

## Preview Questions

1. How do you think life would be different for human beings if they were
half the size they actually are?

2. How would life be different if human beings were twice the size they
actually are?

3. What are the advantages and disadvantages of being short or tall?

## Response Questions

1. What books or movies do you know that play with the idea of a change of
human size?

2. Are there any children's stories in your language that tell about the
adventures of giants or very small people?

3. If you were taller than you are now, what would be the advantages and
disadvantages for you?

4. If you could shrink in size for one day, small enough to observe others
without their noticing you, where would you go and what would you observe?

## Analysis

1. Read the opening paragraph, then close the book and write in your own
words what Gould said about size.

2. A large part of this excerpt is devoted to an imaginary account of what
would happen to a man if he were the size of an ant. Gould presents this
account as evidence for an important point that he wants to make. What is
that point? Does the example of the ant-sized man help the reader
understand the point?

3. If you were asked to choose one sentence from this excerpt that contains
in it the key idea of the whole passage, which sentence would you select?

**WHITE LIES: Ronald Adler, Lawrence Rosenfeld, and Neil Towne**

The excerpt is taken from the third edition of a college textbook used in communications courses: Interplay: The Process of Interpersonal Communication.

## Preview Questions

1. When was the last time you told a lie? What was it?

2. When was the last time you think somebody told you a lie? What were the circumstances?

3. Is it ever justifiable to tell a lie?

4. Do you know what a white lie is? If you don't, can you guess? How is the concept expressed in your language?

## Response Questions

1. Were you surprised to read that the authors thought that white lies could be helpful? Why or why not?

2. How appropriate did it seem to you to be reading about lies in a textbook devoted to the idea of communication?

3. Which of the five motives discussed seemed to you to be the most acceptable?

## Analysis

1. The authors give five motives for lying. How many paragraphs do they use to discuss these five motives?

2. Make an outline showing the main idea of each paragraph in the section headed "Motives for Lying."

3. How many paragraphs do the authors use to introduce the discussion of the motives for lying? What information do those paragraphs provide—and how useful is that for the reader to appreciate the discussion of the motives?

4. This excerpt from a book could also stand separately as an essay on "White Lies." What it lacks, though, is a conclusion; right now the argument stops dead after the discussion of the five motives. What do you think would make a good concluding paragraph?

5. The authors mention some specific examples in their discussion of motives. What evidence do they cite beyond their own opinions?

**THE BASIC—NONBASIC CONCEPT:** Donald Steila, Douglas Wilms, and Edward P. Leahy

This excerpt is taken from a textbook used in college geography courses.

## Preview Questions

1. What are the industries and specialties of a city you know well?

2. What happens to an area when a natural resource (for example, oil, coal, gold, fish) either runs out or is no longer in demand? Do you know of any areas where this has happened?

3. Can you name cities that are famous for having a particular industry to support them?

## Response Questions

1. What "nonbasic" services do you and your family use on a weekly basis?

2. Would you prefer to work in a basic or a nonbasic industry? What are your reasons?

3. If a basic industry goes, does a community necessarily have to collapse and become a ghost town? What other alternatives are there?

4. Can you provide any additional analogies to demonstrate the concept of basic and nonbasic industries?

## Analysis

1. The excerpt consists of three paragraphs. The first paragraph introduces the concept of basic and nonbasic industries. What is the focus of the other two paragraphs?

2. What questions would you have for the authors if you read only the first sentence of the excerpt?

3. How many examples do the authors give to help you understand the concepts of (a) basic and (b) nonbasic industries? What are they? Do the examples help your understanding of the concepts?

4. Paragraph three is devoted to one long and detailed imaginary illustration of the concept of basic and nonbasic industries. Would the concept be as clear to you without that illustration? Why do you think the authors chose a hypothetical and not a real example?

5. Where do the authors bring themselves in as an example? What effect does their bringing themselves in have on you as a reader? Why do you think they refer to themselves as "The authors of this text" and not as "we"?

67

ECONOMICS AND SCARCITY: Patrick J. Welch and Gerry F. Welch

This excerpt is taken from a college-level economics textbook.

Preview Questions

1.  Do you have enough financial resources for the things you want to buy?
What things do you want that you can't afford?

2. Do you ever have to make decisions to buy one thing instead of another
because you can't afford both?  What items have you had to make these
decisions about?

3. If someone gave you $500 to spend today, in one day, how would you spend
it?

Response Questions

1. Have you ever studied or would you like to study economics? Why or why
not? What does economics deal with?  What applications does the subject
have to jobs and careers?

2. Would you have chosen the book or the date? Why? What image would you
have of a person who chose the opposite?

3. Lines 9-10 in the reading passage say that "societies face the same
scarcity problem [as individuals] on a larger scale." What scarcity
problems can you think of facing societies in the world today?

4. What do you think your family would do with $1,000 won in a lottery? How
might that be different from what you would do with it if you had the sole
choice?

5. What economic tradeoffs do people in your country face?

Analysis

1. The first paragraph contains three questions. Do you think the passage
would be improved if statements were used instead of questions (You might
not own the car you would most enjoy. You might not have...etc.)? Why or
why not?

2. The authors begin with the abstract concept of scarcity in economics.
How do they explain to you what the concept means in economic terms? Is
their explanation clear?

3. Which parts of this excerpt are the most memorable? That is, what parts
do you think you might remember in a week's time?

4. What is the focus of paragraph five? If you had to give it a heading of
a few words, what would you write?

5. What is the focus of the sixth paragraph?  In other words, what is the

paragraph about? And what example do the authors give to explain and illustrate the main idea of the paragraph? What examples of your own could you add to that paragraph?

Printed in the United States
by Bookmasters

Printed in the United States
By Bookmasters